Growth Mindset Prayer Journal

THIS JOURNAL BELONGS TO:

DEDICATED TO MY LATE
GRAND AUNT (AUNTIE WINNIE)
WHO PRAYED FOR ME DAY
AND NIGHT.

TABLE OF CONTENTS

Introduction

Growth Mindset Prayer Journal

Purpose of the Journal

Why You Should Pray

Reasons to Pray

What the Bible Says About Prayer

Key Biblical Teachings on Prayer

TABLE OF CONTENTS

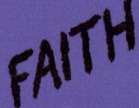

Sometimes it's tricky to find the right words to say when you want to pray. That's why I made this prayer journal just for you! Remember, you can talk to God anytime, anywhere, and as much as you want. God is super powerful, knows everything, and is always right there with you.

In this journal, you'll find spots to write your own prayers. But if you don't know what to say yet, don't worry, there are some prayers here to help you get started.

I made this journal to help you grow your faith and believe in yourself more every day. My great Aunt always told me how important prayer is. She would say, "Mi love yuh and mi pray fi yuh day an nite," which means "I love you and I pray for you every day and every night."

I hope you pray a lot, day and night!

- Symonette Hibbert

Here's a little rhyme to keep in mind:
"When words are hard and prayers are few,
Just open this book. God's listening to you!"

Here are some great reasons why you should pray:

Talk to God:
Prayer helps you chat with God about your thoughts, feelings, and what you need.

Feel Calm:
Praying can make you feel peaceful and less worried when things get tough.

Get Help:
When you don't know what to do, prayer can help you find good answers and make smart choices.

Be Together:
Praying with friends and family helps everyone feel closer and supported.

Say Thanks:
Prayer reminds you to be thankful and think about all the good things in your life.

Here's a little rhyme to end your day:

Prayer is a gift, both big and small,
Talk to God anytime , He hears it all!

What the Bible Says About Prayer

1. **Talking to God:** The Bible tells us prayer is how we talk with God. Philippians 4:6-7 says we can ask God for anything and He will give us peace.

2. **Believe and Trust:** In Mark 11:24, Jesus says when you pray, believe that God will answer, and it will happen!

3. **Keep Praying:** Luke 18:1 teaches us to never stop praying, even if it takes time.

4. **Saying Sorry and Forgiving:** James 5:16 says praying helps us heal and forgive each other when we say sorry.

5. **Praying for Others:** The Bible shows us that praying for other people, like in 1 Timothy 2:1, is very important.

Here's a little rhyme to remember:

Prayer is talking, prayer is care,

God loves to listen everywhere!

7

Growth Mindset Prayer

Heavenly Father ,

I come before You with a grateful heart. Thank You for the gift of life and the chance to grow a little more each day. Please help me to see challenges not as roadblocks but as opportunities to become stronger and wiser. When I stumble, remind me that failure is not the end , it is a chance to learn and try again.

Fill me with resilience and courage Lord, so I can keep going even when things feel hard. Help me celebrate every bit of progress, no matter how small, and find joy in the journey of learning and becoming better.

As Your Word says in Philippians 4:13: "I can do all things through Christ who strengthens me." Please help me to lean on Your wisdom and strength, knowing that with You by my side, I can face anything.

Keep my thoughts positive and my heart open to new possibilities. Teach me to reflect Your love in all I do, so I can inspire and uplift those around me as we grow together.

Thank You for being my constant source of love, strength, and support. Thank you for all that you have done, all that you are doing and all that you are about to do . Amen.

My personal prayer

_____

_____

_____

_____

_____

_____

_____

_____

_____

_____

_____

_____

_____

_____

_____

_____

Therefore I tell you, whatever you ask for in prayer, believe that you have received it, and it will be yours. - Mark 11:24

Growth Mindset Prayer for my Teachers

Dear God,

Thank You for my teacher and for the time and care they give to help me learn and grow. Please bless them with strength, patience, and wisdom every day. Help them to feel encouraged, even when the days are long and challenging. When things get tough, remind them that they are making a difference in my life and the lives of my classmates. Let them see the impact of their kindness and hard work. Help them to stay strong, just like Philippians 4:13 says, "I can do all things through Christ who strengthens me."

Please fill our classroom with joy, curiosity, and respect. Let it be a place where we feel safe, supported, and excited to learn. Help my teacher to see their own amazing potential, just as they help us see ours.

Thank You for guiding them each step of the way. May their efforts leave a lasting impact, and may they always know how much they are appreciated.

Amen.

My personal prayer

_____

_____

_____

_____

_____

_____

_____

_____

_____

_____

_____

_____

_____

_____

_____

_____

_____

Therefore I tell you, whatever you ask for in prayer, believe that you have received it, and it will be yours. - Mark 11:24

Growth Mindset Prayer for my Principal

Dear God,

Thank You for my principal and for the hard work he/she does to make our school a great place to learn and grow. Please give him/her courage to face challenges, patience to handle each day, and wisdom to make good decisions for our school.

Help him/her to be strong and to keep going, even when things are tough. Remind him/her that every effort he/she makes helps us all. Let our school be a place where everyone feels safe, valued, and excited to learn.

As Philippians 4:13 says, "I can do all things through Christ who strengthens me." May this promise give him/her confidence and remind him/her that You are always with him/her.

Thank You for blessing us with a leader who cares for us. Please continue to guide him/her, support him/her, and fill him/her with joy as he/she helps us grow.

Amen.

My personal prayer

_____

_____

_____

_____

_____

_____

_____

_____

_____

_____

_____

_____

_____

_____

_____

_____

Therefore I tell you, whatever you ask for in prayer, believe that you have received it, and it will be yours. - Mark 11:24

Growth Mindset Prayer for My Friend

Dear God,

Today, I pray for my friend. Please give (Name) the courage and strength to face anything that comes their way. Help (Name) to see every challenge as a chance to get stronger and to remember Your promise in Philippians 4:13, "I can do all things through Christ who gives me strength."

When things don't go the way we hoped, help (Name) to see it's not the end, but just a step toward something better. Remind (Name) of James 1:2, that hard times can help us grow, be patient, and become the best we can be.

God, please surround my friend with love, encouragement, and positive thoughts. When they feel unsure, help them remember Jeremiah 29:11, "I know the plans I have for you, plans to make you prosper and not to harm you, plans to give you hope and a future."

Let (Name) wake up each day ready to learn, grow, and be their best. Thank You for giving me such a special friend. Help us to always cheer each other on and walk together in Your love. Thank You for all that You have done, all that You are doing, and all that You are about to do. Amen.

My personal prayer

_____

_____

_____

_____

_____

_____

_____

_____

_____

_____

_____

_____

_____

_____

_____

_____

Therefore I tell you, whatever you ask for in prayer, believe that you have received it, and it will be yours. - Mark 11:24

Growth Mindset Prayer for my Mom

Dear God,

Thank You so much for giving me my mom. I'm really thankful for her love, her smart advice, and how she makes everyone around her feel special.

Please help her see every hard time as a chance to get stronger and learn something new. Remind her, like You say in Matthew 19:26, that with You, anything is possible. When life feels too busy or stressful, please give her a calm and happy heart.

Help her remember Philippians 4:13, "I can do all things through Christ who gives me strength," so she knows You're always with her. Please give her the courage to follow her dreams and the joy to keep going, even when things are tough.

Surround her with people who love and support her, and let her shine Your love everywhere she goes. Help her keep growing in faith, wisdom, and strength, knowing that Your plan for her is always good.

Thank you for all that You have done, all that You are doing, and all that You are about to do. Amen.

My personal prayer

_____

_____

_____

_____

_____

_____

_____

_____

_____

_____

_____

_____

_____

_____

_____

_____

_____

Therefore I tell you, whatever you ask for in prayer, believe that you
have received it, and it will be yours. - Mark 11:24

Growth Mindset Prayer for My Dad

Heavenly Father ,

Thank You for my dad. He's such a blessing in my life, and I'm so glad You made him my dad. Please help him always have a growth mindset, so he can see every challenge as a chance to get better and learn new things. When things feel hard, remind him of Philippians 4:13, "I can do all things through Christ who gives me strength," so he knows You are always with him. Help him remember that even if he falls or makes mistakes, like it says in Proverbs 24:16, he can get back up and keep trying. Please give him courage to try new things, even if they feel scary at first. When he feels worried, remind him of Isaiah 41:10, "Do not be afraid, for I am with you," so he knows he's never alone.

Fill his heart with joy and strength, and help him keep going even when things are tough. Let him be proud of every little step forward and let his life inspire others to keep growing too.

Thank You for my amazing dad and for all the ways he teaches me and loves me. Thank you for all that You have done, all that You are doing, and all that You are about to do. Amen.

My personal prayer

Therefore I tell you, whatever you ask for in prayer, believe that you have received it, and it will be yours. - Mark 11:24

Growth Mindset Prayer for My Sister

Almighty Father,

Thank You so much for my sister. She is such a special gift, and I'm so glad You made her my sister. Thank You for all the amazing talents and gifts You've put inside her. Please help her believe in herself and remember that she can do great things with You by her side.

When things are hard, remind her of Philippians 4:13, "I can do all things through Christ who gives me strength." Help her try new things, even if they feel a little scary, and to see mistakes as chances to learn and grow.

Please give her courage, joy, and a happy heart. When she stumbles, help her get back up and keep going. Remind her that she is fearfully and wonderfully made, just like it says in Psalm 139:14, and that You made her journey special just for her.

Surround her with people who love and encourage her. Help her celebrate even the little wins and trust that You have an amazing plan for her, like Jeremiah 29:11 says.

Thank You for giving me such an awesome sister. Thank you for all that You have done, all that You are doing, and all that You are about to do. Amen.

My personal prayer

_____

_____

_____

_____

_____

_____

_____

_____

_____

_____

_____

_____

_____

_____

_____

_____

Therefore I tell you, whatever you ask for in prayer, believe that you
have received it, and it will be yours. - Mark 11:24

Growth Mindset Prayer for My Brother

Oh Heavenly Father,

Thank You so much for my brother. I'm really grateful for him and for the way You made him special. Please give him Your strength and guide him every day. Help him to be brave when things get hard and to remember that challenges are chances to grow.

Remind him of Philippians 4:13, "I can do all things through Christ who gives me strength," so he knows he can trust You no matter what. Give him a learning heart, like Proverbs 1:5 says, "Let the wise hear and increase in learning," so he sees every mistake as a step toward success.

Please help him grow in both his heart and his faith, always walking on the path You have planned for him. When things don't go right, give him the strength to get back up and try again. Surround him with people who love and encourage him, and let him feel You with him every step of the way.

Thank You for the wonderful plans You have for him, plans to give him hope and a bright future like Jeremiah 29:11 says. Thank you for all that You have done, all that You are doing, and all that You are about to do. Amen.

My personal prayer

_____

_____

_____

_____

_____

_____

_____

_____

_____

_____

_____

_____

_____

_____

_____

Therefore I tell you, whatever you ask for in prayer, believe that you
have received it, and it will be yours. - Mark 11:24

Growth Mindset Prayer for My Grandmother

Almighty Father,

Thank You so much for my grandma. I'm so thankful for her wisdom, her strength, and all the ways she makes our lives better. Please fill her heart with joy, peace, and the courage to keep learning and trying new things.

Remind her of Isaiah 40:31, "Those who hope in the Lord will renew their strength," so she knows You will help her feel strong every day. Let her see each new day as a chance to enjoy life, learn something new, and smile at the little blessings You give.

Help her always be thankful, just like it says in 1 Thessalonians 5:16-18, "Rejoice always, pray continually, give thanks in all circumstances." Let her thank You for the big and small things and inspire others to be grateful too.

Remind her of Proverbs 16:31, "Gray hair is a crown of splendor," and help her wear her years with pride, knowing they show a life full of love and faith.

Please give her hope for the future, peace in her heart, and excitement for what's still to come. Thank You for the gift of my amazing grandma. Thank you for all that You have done, all that You are doing, and all that You are about to do. Amen.

My personal prayer

_____

_____

_____

_____

_____

_____

_____

_____

_____

_____

_____

_____

_____

_____

_____

_____

Therefore I tell you, whatever you ask for in prayer, believe that you have received it, and it will be yours. - Mark 11:24

Growth Mindset Prayer for My Grandfather

Dear Heavenly Father,

Thank You for my grandpa. I'm really thankful for his love, his wisdom, and all the ways he helps our family. Please fill him with peace and give him new strength every day.

Remind him of Isaiah 40:31, "Those who hope in the Lord will renew their strength. They will soar on wings like eagles." Help him feel strong and brave, knowing You are always with him.

Please help him keep learning and growing, seeing every challenge as a chance to get better and understand more.

Fill his heart with hope and trust in Your plan. Help him know that growing older is a special gift full of chances to do great things.

Thank You for my grandpa and for all the ways he shows Your love. Help him keep growing with courage and hope. Thank You for all that You have done, all that You are doing, and all that You are about to do. Amen.

My personal prayer

_____

_____

_____

_____

_____

_____

_____

_____

_____

_____

_____

_____

_____

_____

_____

_____

_____

Therefore I tell you, whatever you ask for in prayer, believe that you have received it, and it will be yours. - Mark 11:24

Growth Mindset Prayer for My Stepmom

Almighty God,

Thank You for my stepmom. I'm so happy she's part of my life and for all the love and care she shows. Please fill her heart with Your peace and give her strength to keep growing. Help her see every challenge as a chance to get closer to You. Remind her of Philippians 4:13, "I can do all things through Christ who gives me strength," so she knows You are always helping her.

Please help her trust You with all her heart, just like Proverbs 3:5-6 says, "Trust in the Lord with all your heart and He will guide your path." Let her feel You guiding her every step. Give her courage and hope. When things get hard, help her see it as a chance to learn and get stronger. Please open her mind and heart to new ideas and possibilities.

Thank You for the special path You have for my stepmom. Surround her with Your love and help her keep growing every day. Thank You for all that You have done, all that You are doing, and all that You are about to do. Amen.

My personal prayer

_____

_____

_____

_____

_____

_____

_____

_____

_____

_____

_____

_____

_____

_____

_____

_____

_____

Therefore I tell you, whatever you ask for in prayer, believe that you have received it, and it will be yours. - Mark 11:24

Growth Mindset Prayer for My Stepdad

Dear Lord,

Thank You for my stepdad and for all the love and guidance he gives me. Please bless him with a heart that wants to grow stronger and never give up.

Help him to see hard times as chances to get better, just like Your Word says in James 1:2-4: "Consider it pure joy, my brothers and sisters, whenever you face trials of many kinds, because you know that the testing of your faith produces perseverance."

May he find joy and strength as he keeps going. Please give him courage to try new things and remind him of Matthew 19:26, "With God, all things are possible." Help him know that even when things get tough, he is never alone.

Surround him with people who cheer him on, and help him see how special he is. Let him remember Psalm 139:14, "I praise You because I am fearfully and wonderfully made."

Thank You for the amazing man he is and for the journey he is on. Help him keep growing and inspiring others with Your love and wisdom.

Thank You for all that You have done, all that You are doing, and all that You are about to do. Amen.

My personal prayer

_____

_____

_____

_____

_____

_____

_____

_____

_____

_____

_____

_____

_____

_____

_____

_____

Therefore I tell you, whatever you ask for in prayer, believe that you have received it, and it will be yours. - Mark 11:24

BE ENCOURAGED

There are going to be days when you feel overwhelmed .

Here's what to say:
Grow with every challenge, learn something new,
Every small step is strength showing through!
"Be transformed by a fresh, new mind," Romans 12:2,
keep that in mind!

Believe in the power of the word "yet."
With God, all things happen, don't you forget!
"With God, all things are possible," Matthew 19:26, that's
unstoppable!

Step outside your comfort and be brave each day.
Keep trying and growing, you're finding your way!
"Let perseverance finish its work," James 1:4,

Keep going strong, there's so much in store!
Faith and growth go hand in hand.
You can do anything with God's strong hand!
"I can do all things through Christ," Philippians 4:13, He's
your might!

Things I am grateful for:

_____

_____

_____

_____

_____

_____

_____

_____

_____

_____

_____

_____

_____

_____

_____

Therefore I tell you, whatever you ask for in prayer, believe that you
have received it, and it will be yours. - Mark 11:24

Growth Mindset Prayer for a Family Member

Dear Heavenly Father,

I come to You with hope for (Name). Please help him/her have a growth mindset, so he/she can face challenges and see mistakes as chances to learn and grow.

Help him/her remember Philippians 4:13, "I can do all things through Christ who gives me strength." May he/she feel Your help and know that with You, he/she can overcome anything.

Please give him/her a strong spirit to keep going, like James 1:2-4 says, "Be happy when you have hard times, because they help you learn to be patient and strong." Let him/her find joy in the journey, knowing each step is part of Your plan.

Surround him/her with Your love and remind him/her of Romans 12:2, "Don't copy what the world does, but change by thinking in a new way." Help him/her to think new thoughts and see all the good things ahead.

Thank You, God, for the amazing potential You gave him/her. Please guide and encourage him/her as he/she grows.

Thank You for all that You have done, all that You are doing, and all that You are about to do. Amen.

My personal prayer

_____

_____

_____

_____

_____

_____

_____

_____

_____

_____

_____

_____

_____

_____

_____

Therefore I tell you, whatever you ask for in prayer, believe that you
have received it, and it will be yours. - Mark 11:24

Growth Mindset Prayer about forgiveness

Heavenly Father,

Please help me learn to forgive, even when it feels hard. Help me let go of hurt feelings and be kind in my heart. Your Word says in Luke 6:28, "Bless those who hurt you, and pray for those who are mean to you." Please help me do this, even when it's really tough.

Teach me to say sorry when I make mistakes, and to say "I forgive you" when others hurt me. Help me remember that forgiving makes my heart happy and free.

I know (Name) might be having a hard time too. Please help him/her and heal their heart. Help me be kind and loving, just like You want me to be.

Thank You for forgiving me every day and for loving me no matter what. Please help me be brave and show forgiveness like You do.

Thank You for all that You have done, all that You are doing, and all that You are about to do. Amen.

My personal prayer

_____

_____

_____

_____

_____

_____

_____

_____

_____

_____

_____

_____

_____

_____

_____

_____

_____

Therefore I tell you, whatever you ask for in prayer, believe that you have received it, and it will be yours. - Mark 11:24

Parents Arguing or Going Through Divorce

Dear God,

It makes me feel sad and worried when my parents argue. Sometimes I do not know what to do, and I just wish things could go back to the way they were. Please help them talk kindly to each other and work through their problems. Remind me of Psalm 34:18: "The Lord is close to the brokenhearted and saves those who are crushed in spirit."

Help me to remember that no matter what happens, You love me, You see me, and You have a plan for my life. Teach me to focus on what I can control, like being kind, helping at home, and sharing my feelings in a respectful way. When things feel uncertain, give me peace in my heart and help me believe that You can bring good out of even hard situations.

Thank You for always being with me and helping me grow stronger. Thank You for all that You have done, all that You are doing, and all that You are about to do. Amen.

My personal prayer

_____

_____

_____

_____

_____

_____

_____

_____

_____

_____

_____

_____

_____

_____

_____

Therefore I tell you, whatever you ask for in prayer, believe that you have received it, and it will be yours. - Mark 11:24

Growth Mindset Prayer for Peer Pressure

Dear Heavenly Father,

Thank You for loving me and always being by my side. Sometimes, I feel pressured by others to do things I'm not sure about. Please help me be strong and make good choices, even when it's hard.

Help me remember what Your Word says in Romans 12:2, "Do not be like the world, but be changed by the renewing of your mind." Please help me think for myself and do what's right, even if others don't.

Give me courage like in Joshua 1:9, "Be strong and courageous. Do not be afraid; do not be discouraged, for the Lord your God will be with you wherever you go."

Help me stand up for what I believe and say no when I need to. Please fill my heart with confidence and remind me that I am fearfully and wonderfully made (Psalm 139:14). Help me know that I do not need to do things just to fit in because You made me special just the way I am.

Thank You for helping me make good choices and for loving me no matter what. Please keep guiding me every day.

Thank You for all that You have done, all that You are doing, and all that You are about to do. Amen.

My personal prayer

_____

_____

_____

_____

_____

_____

_____

_____

_____

_____

_____

_____

_____

_____

_____

_____

Therefore I tell you, whatever you ask for in prayer, believe that you have received it, and it will be yours. - Mark 11:24

Growth Mindset Prayer for Body confidence

Dear Heavenly Father,

Thank You for creating me in Your image and making me wonderfully unique. When I feel insecure about my body, remind me of Your truth in Psalm 139:14, that I am fearfully and wonderfully made. Help me to focus on developing a kind and courageous heart, as 1 Samuel 16:7 teaches, knowing that You value what's inside more than outward appearance.

When I compare myself to others or feel inadequate, give me the strength to shift my focus and embrace challenges as opportunities to grow. Help me to silence negative thoughts and replace them with words of truth and confidence. Teach me to treat my body with love and care, celebrating every small victory along the way.

Lord, when I stumble, remind me that I am a work in progress. Strengthen my faith and develop within me a growth mindset that sees mistakes as lessons and setbacks as opportunities. Help me to trust that, with You by my side, I will continue to grow into the person You've created me to be.

Thank You for loving me unconditionally and for seeing the best in me. Help me to see myself through Your eyes; with grace, love, and compassion.

Thank you for all that you have done, all that you are doing and all that you are about to do. Amen.

My personal prayer

_____

_____

_____

_____

_____

_____

_____

_____

_____

_____

_____

_____

_____

_____

_____

_____

Therefore I tell you, whatever you ask for in prayer, believe that you
have received it, and it will be yours. - Mark 11:24

Growth Mindset Prayer for Difficult Times

Dear Most loving God,

Right now, things feel really hard and I don't know what to do. But I know You are with me, even when I'm scared or sad.

Please help me see hard times as a way to grow stronger and learn more about You and myself. When I feel worried or unsure, remind me of Isaiah 41:10: "So do not fear, for I am with you; do not be dismayed, for I am your God. I will strengthen you and help you; I will hold you up with my strong right hand."

Please give me the strength to keep going, even when I want to give up. Help me be patient with myself and learn from my mistakes. Your Word in James 1:2-4 tells me to be happy when things are hard, because those hard times help me grow strong and patient. Please help me trust You and find joy even in challenges.

I believe You have a plan for me, even if I can't see it now. Thank You for always being with me and for giving me strength. Philippians 4:13 says, "I can do all things through Christ who gives me strength."

Today, I give my life to You and ask You to guide me every step.Thank You for all You have done, all You are doing, and all You are about to do. Amen.

My personal prayer

_____

_____

_____

_____

_____

_____

_____

_____

_____

_____

_____

_____

_____

_____

_____

_____

Therefore I tell you, whatever you ask for in prayer, believe that you
have received it, and it will be yours. - Mark 11:24

Growth Mindset Graduation Prayer

Dear Heavenly Father,

Thank You for bringing me to this special day. I am so grateful for every part of my journey ; the late nights studying, the friends who helped me, and even the mistakes that taught me to keep going. I know You were with me through it all.

As I think about the future, please give me courage to face whatever comes next. Help me remember that You are always by my side, even when I'm not sure what to do.

Please help me love learning and growing. When I face hard things, help me see them as chances to get better and stronger. When I fall, give me the strength to get back up, knowing that with You, all things are possible.

Keep my mind open and my heart ready to learn. Help me ask questions and listen to the wisdom You and others give me. Let me never think I know everything.

Please guide me when I have to make big choices. Help me pick the right paths that honor You and use the gifts You gave me to help others.

When I feel worried or doubt myself, remind me of what You said in Jeremiah 29:11: "For I know the plans I have for you," says the Lord. "Plans to prosper you and not to harm you, plans to give you hope and a future." Thank You for bringing me here today. I trust You with my future and want my life to show Your love and goodness.

Thank You for all that You have done, all that You are doing, and all that You are about to do. Amen.

My personal prayer

_____

_____

_____

_____

_____

_____

_____

_____

_____

_____

_____

_____

_____

_____

_____

Therefore I tell you, whatever you ask for in prayer, believe that you have received it, and it will be yours. - Mark 11:24

Growth Mindset Prayer for Embracing Opportunities

Dear Heavenly Father,

I come to You with a mix of excitement and nerves. Thank You for the opportunities You have placed before me. When I feel overwhelmed, remind me of Your promise in Jeremiah 29:11: "For I know the plans I have for you," declares the Lord, "plans to prosper you and not to harm you, plans to give you hope and a future."

Give me courage, Lord, to step into the unknown. When I am afraid, help me to remember 2 Timothy 1:7: "For God has not given us a spirit of fear, but of power and of love and of a sound mind." Let me see challenges as opportunities to grow, not roadblocks. Open my eyes to the possibilities around me. Grant me wisdom in my decisions, as James 1:5 encourages: "If any of you lacks wisdom, you should ask God, who gives generously to all without finding fault, and it will be given to you."

In everything, let me reflect Your love. I may not know where these opportunities will lead, but I trust in Your guidance, as Proverbs 3:5-6 teaches: "Trust in the Lord with all your heart and lean not on your own understanding; but in all your ways acknowledge him, and he shall direct thy path."

Thank You for believing in me and for walking with me on this journey. Thank you for all that you have done, all that you are doing and all that you are about to do. Amen.

My personal prayer

_____

_____

_____

_____

_____

_____

_____

_____

_____

_____

_____

_____

_____

_____

_____

_____

Therefore I tell you, whatever you ask for in prayer, believe that you
have received it, and it will be yours. - Mark 11:24

Growth Mindset Prayer for Grief

Heavenly Father,

My heart feels so heavy, and sometimes the sadness feels like too much. I need You, God. Please give me comfort and strength. When I cry, remind me that You see my tears and that You care about my pain. Hold me close because I need You more than ever right now. Your Word says in Psalm 34:18, "The Lord is close to the brokenhearted and saves those who are crushed in spirit." Help me feel You near me, especially when I feel all alone.

Sometimes I wonder if I will ever feel happy again. Please remind me that this sadness won't last forever and that there is still hope ahead. Give me the strength to keep going, one step and one day at a time. Even though I don't understand why this happened, I trust You, Lord. Remind me of Romans 8:28; that You can bring good out of everything for those who love You.

Please give me courage for each day. When I feel weak, be my strength. When I feel lost, guide me. And when I feel alone, remind me that You are always with me. Help me to be patient with myself as I go through this time of grief.

Father, show me how to honor the memory of what I have lost while still finding ways to move forward. Help me notice even the smallest moments of peace and joy in the middle of my sadness.

Thank You for Your love that never leaves me, even in my hardest moments. Thank you guiding me through this moment dear Father. Thank you for all that you have done, all that you are doing and all that you are about to do. Amen.

My personal prayer

_____

_____

_____

_____

_____

_____

_____

_____

_____

_____

_____

_____

_____

_____

_____

Therefore I tell you, whatever you ask for in prayer, believe that you
have received it, and it will be yours. - Mark 11:24

Growth Mindset Prayer for Consistency

Dear Heavenly Father,

I come to You today asking for Your help to be steady and consistent. Thank You for giving me chances every day to do my best, practice good habits, and keep working toward the special purpose You have for me.

Sometimes it's hard to keep going when things feel slow or tough. Please give me strength to keep moving forward, one step at a time, and remind me that You are always by my side.

When I feel like giving up, help me remember that every small effort matters and brings me closer to the good things You have planned. Remind me of Your words in Hebrews 12:11; that even though discipline isn't always fun, it helps me grow stronger and brings peace later on.

Lord, help me stay focused on what really matters. Teach me to commit my plans, goals, and daily actions to You, just like it says in Proverbs 16:3. I know that if I give everything to You, You will guide my steps.

Fill me with courage, patience, and a growth mindset so that I don't just start well but also finish strong. Let my life show others how faithful You are, because with You, nothing is impossible. Thank you for all that you have done, all that you are doing and all that you are about to do. Amen.

My personal prayer

_____

_____

_____

_____

_____

_____

_____

_____

_____

_____

_____

_____

_____

_____

Therefore I tell you, whatever you ask for in prayer, believe that you
have received it, and it will be yours. - Mark 11:24

Growth Mindset Prayer to Strengthen My Faith

Dear Heavenly Father,

I come to You today with an open heart, wanting to know You better and trust You more. Thank You for always loving me, guiding me, and being patient with me. Please help me to have a strong faith that stays with me no matter what happens.

Remind me of Hebrews 11:1: "Faith means being sure about what we hope for, and certain of what we do not see." Even when I don't know what will happen next, help me trust that You are working things out for my good.

When I feel scared or worried, remind me of 2 Corinthians 5:7: "We walk by faith, not by sight." Give me courage to take steps forward, not because I know everything, but because I know You are always with me.

When I feel tired or weak, let me remember Isaiah 40:31: "Those who hope in the Lord will get new strength. They will soar like eagles, run and not get tired, walk and not be weak." Please help me keep going and never give up.

When my faith feels small, remind me of Matthew 17:20: "If you have faith as small as a mustard seed, you can move mountains." Show me that little faith can do big things when I trust You.

Help me see tough times as chances to grow stronger and closer to You. Teach me to face challenges with courage, knowing that You are helping me every step of the way.

Lord, I want my faith to show in how I treat others, with love, kindness, and hope. Thank You for all You have done, all You are doing, and all You will do. Amen.

My personal prayer

_____

_____

_____

_____

_____

_____

_____

_____

_____

_____

_____

_____

_____

_____

_____

Therefore I tell you, whatever you ask for in prayer, believe that you have received it, and it will be yours. - Mark 11:24

Changes in Living Situations (Moving to a New Home or School)

Dear God,

Change can feel scary because it is different from what I am used to. Sometimes I worry about making new friends, learning my way around, or fitting in. But I know You are with me. Your Word says in Joshua 1:9: "Be strong and courageous. Do not be afraid, do not be discouraged, for the Lord your God will be with you wherever you go." Help me to see this change as an opportunity to grow, learn new things, and meet people who can make my life better.

Remind me that I can take small steps every day to feel more comfortable, and that mistakes are part of learning. Please give me courage when I feel nervous and joy when I notice the good things in this new place.

Thank You for guiding me and helping me become braver through this experience. Thank You for all that You have done, all that You are doing, and all that You are about to do. Amen.

My personal prayer

_____

_____

_____

_____

_____

_____

_____

_____

_____

_____

_____

_____

_____

_____

_____

Therefore I tell you, whatever you ask for in prayer, believe that you
have received it, and it will be yours. - Mark 11:24

My personal prayer

_____

_____

_____

_____

_____

_____

_____

_____

_____

_____

_____

_____

_____

_____

_____

_____

_____

Therefore I tell you, whatever you ask for in prayer, believe that you
have received it, and it will be yours. - Mark 11:24

My personal prayer

_____

_____

_____

_____

_____

_____

_____

_____

_____

_____

_____

_____

_____

_____

_____

_____

Therefore I tell you, whatever you ask for in prayer, believe that you
have received it, and it will be yours. - Mark 11:24

A New Sibling and Feeling Less Attention

Dear God,

Thank You for blessing our family with my new brother or sister. I know they are a gift, but sometimes I feel like I am not getting as much attention as before. That can make me feel a little left out.

Please help me to remember that I am loved and special to You and to my family. Remind me of Jeremiah 31:3: "I have loved you with an everlasting love; I have drawn you with unfailing kindness." Teach me to be patient when things feel different and to find joy in being a big brother or sister. Show me ways to help and to make happy memories together.

Remind me that love grows, it is not divided, and that this change can teach me to care, share, and be a good example.

Thank You for all that You have done, all that You are doing, and all that You are about to do. Amen.

My personal prayer

_____

_____

_____

_____

_____

_____

_____

_____

_____

_____

_____

_____

_____

_____

_____

_____

_____

Therefore I tell you, whatever you ask for in prayer, believe that you have received it, and it will be yours. - Mark 11:24

My personal prayer

_____

_____

_____

_____

_____

_____

_____

_____

_____

_____

_____

_____

_____

_____

_____

_____

_____

Therefore I tell you, whatever you ask for in prayer, believe that you have received it, and it will be yours. - Mark 11:24

My personal prayer

_____

_____

_____

_____

_____

_____

_____

_____

_____

_____

_____

_____

_____

_____

_____

_____

_____

Therefore I tell you, whatever you ask for in prayer, believe that you have received it, and it will be yours. - Mark 11:24

My personal prayer

_____

_____

_____

_____

_____

_____

_____

_____

_____

_____

_____

_____

_____

_____

_____

_____

Therefore I tell you, whatever you ask for in prayer, believe that you have received it, and it will be yours. - Mark 11:24

My personal prayer

_____

_____

_____

_____

_____

_____

_____

_____

_____

_____

_____

_____

_____

_____

_____

_____

Therefore I tell you, whatever you ask for in prayer, believe that you have received it, and it will be yours. - Mark 11:24

My personal prayer

_____

_____

_____

_____

_____

_____

_____

_____

_____

_____

_____

_____

_____

_____

_____

_____

_____

Therefore I tell you, whatever you ask for in prayer, believe that you have received it, and it will be yours. - Mark 11:24

My personal prayer

_____

_____

_____

_____

_____

_____

_____

_____

_____

_____

_____

_____

_____

_____

_____

_____

Therefore I tell you, whatever you ask for in prayer, believe that you have received it, and it will be yours. - Mark 11:24

My personal prayer

_____

_____

_____

_____

_____

_____

_____

_____

_____

_____

_____

_____

_____

_____

_____

_____

Therefore I tell you, whatever you ask for in prayer, believe that you
have received it, and it will be yours. - Mark 11:24

My personal prayer

_____

_____

_____

_____

_____

_____

_____

_____

_____

_____

_____

_____

_____

_____

_____

_____

Therefore I tell you, whatever you ask for in prayer, believe that you
have received it, and it will be yours. - Mark 11:24

My personal prayer

_____

_____

_____

_____

_____

_____

_____

_____

_____

_____

_____

_____

_____

_____

_____

_____

_____

Therefore I tell you, whatever you ask for in prayer, believe that you
have received it, and it will be yours. - Mark 11:24

My personal prayer

_____

_____

_____

_____

_____

_____

_____

_____

_____

_____

_____

_____

_____

_____

_____

_____

Therefore I tell you, whatever you ask for in prayer, believe that you
have received it, and it will be yours. - Mark 11:24

My personal prayer

_____

_____

_____

_____

_____

_____

_____

_____

_____

_____

_____

_____

_____

_____

_____

_____

Therefore I tell you, whatever you ask for in prayer, believe that you
have received it, and it will be yours. - Mark 11:24

My personal prayer

_____

_____

_____

_____

_____

_____

_____

_____

_____

_____

_____

_____

_____

_____

_____

_____

_____

Therefore I tell you, whatever you ask for in prayer, believe that you
have received it, and it will be yours. - Mark 11:24

My personal prayer

_____

_____

_____

_____

_____

_____

_____

_____

_____

_____

_____

_____

_____

_____

_____

_____

_____

_____

Therefore I tell you, whatever you ask for in prayer, believe that you have received it, and it will be yours. - Mark 11:24

My personal prayer

_____

_____

_____

_____

_____

_____

_____

_____

_____

_____

_____

_____

_____

_____

_____

_____

Therefore I tell you, whatever you ask for in prayer, believe that you
have received it, and it will be yours. - Mark 11:24

My personal prayer

_____

_____

_____

_____

_____

_____

_____

_____

_____

_____

_____

_____

_____

_____

_____

_____

_____

Therefore I tell you, whatever you ask for in prayer, believe that you have received it, and it will be yours. - Mark 11:24

My personal prayer

_____

_____

_____

_____

_____

_____

_____

_____

_____

_____

_____

_____

_____

_____

_____

_____

Therefore I tell you, whatever you ask for in prayer, believe that you
have received it, and it will be yours. - Mark 11:24

My personal prayer

_____

_____

_____

_____

_____

_____

_____

_____

_____

_____

_____

_____

_____

_____

_____

_____

_____

Therefore I tell you, whatever you ask for in prayer, believe that you
have received it, and it will be yours. - Mark 11:24

My personal prayer

_____

_____

_____

_____

_____

_____

_____

_____

_____

_____

_____

_____

_____

_____

_____

Therefore I tell you, whatever you ask for in prayer, believe that you have received it, and it will be yours. - Mark 11:24

My personal prayer

_____
_____
_____
_____
_____
_____
_____
_____
_____
_____
_____
_____
_____
_____
_____
_____
_____

Therefore I tell you, whatever you ask for in prayer, believe that you
have received it, and it will be yours. - Mark 11:24

My personal prayer

_____

_____

_____

_____

_____

_____

_____

_____

_____

_____

_____

_____

_____

_____

_____

_____

_____

Therefore I tell you, whatever you ask for in prayer, believe that you
have received it, and it will be yours. - Mark 11:24

My personal prayer

_____

_____

_____

_____

_____

_____

_____

_____

_____

_____

_____

_____

_____

_____

_____

_____

Therefore I tell you, whatever you ask for in prayer, believe that you
have received it, and it will be yours. - Mark 11:24

My personal prayer

_____

_____

_____

_____

_____

_____

_____

_____

_____

_____

_____

_____

_____

_____

_____

Therefore I tell you, whatever you ask for in prayer, believe that you
have received it, and it will be yours. - Mark 11:24

My personal prayer

_____

_____

_____

_____

_____

_____

_____

_____

_____

_____

_____

_____

_____

_____

_____

_____

_____

Therefore I tell you, whatever you ask for in prayer, believe that you have received it, and it will be yours. - Mark 11:24

My personal prayer

_____

_____

_____

_____

_____

_____

_____

_____

_____

_____

_____

_____

_____

_____

_____

_____

_____

Therefore I tell you, whatever you ask for in prayer, believe that you
have received it, and it will be yours. - Mark 11:24

Activity 1:
My Growth Shield Protecting My Mindset

What You Will Need: Pencil, crayons, or markers

What to Do:

Draw a big shield on your page.
Divide the shield into 4 sections.
In each section, write or draw something that protects your growth mindset (like prayer, positive thoughts, family support, scripture, or trying again).

Add a short prayer:

"Dear God, please help me use my shield when I feel weak or discouraged. Amen."

Remember: God gives you strength to protect your heart and mind from doubt.

87

Activity 2:

"Gratitude Garden" Planting Thankful Seeds

What You Will Need:
Paper, crayons, or stickers

What to Do:
1. Draw a garden with flowers or trees.
2. On each flower, write something you are thankful for (family, friends, talents, school, God's love).
3. Under each flower, write a short prayer of thanks.
4. Example: "Thank You God for my family who loves me."

Remember: Gratitude helps your heart grow like a beautiful garden.

89

Activity 3:

"Courage Badges" Celebrating Brave Moments

What You Will Need:
Pencil, markers, or colorful paper

What to Do:

1. Draw 3–5 circle "badges" on the page.
2. In each badge, write something brave you have done (like trying something new, speaking up, forgiving, or being kind).
3. Add a prayer on top:
4. "Dear God, thank You for helping me be brave. Please help me keep growing in courage."
5. Decorate your badges with colors, stars, or symbols that remind you of strength.

Remember: Every act of courage is a victory worth celebrating!

Activity 4:
"God's Promise Backpack" – Carrying Strength With Me

What You Will Need:

Pencil, crayons, or markers

What to Do:

1. Draw a backpack on your page.
2. Inside the backpack, write or draw "tools" you want to carry with you, like:
   - 📖 Bible verse
   - 💜 Kindness
   - 💪 Courage
   - 🙏 Prayer
   - 😊 Positivity
3. Write a prayer:
4. "Dear God, thank You for filling my backpack with everything I need to grow and be strong."

Remember: With God's promises in your "backpack," you are always prepared for challenges.

Activity 5:
"Turn It Around" Turning Challenges into Prayers

What You will need:

Your prayer journal and a pencil or crayons

What to Do:
Think of a Challenge
Write or draw about something that feels hard or scary right now. It could be a problem at school, learning something new, or feeling nervous about trying.

Turn Your Challenge Into a Prayer
Write a prayer asking God to help you stay strong, brave, and keep trying even when things are tough.

Here is a starter you can use:
"Dear God, help me to keep going even when it's hard. Help me believe I can grow and learn every day. Amen."

Say Your Prayer Out Loud
Practice saying your prayer anytime you feel worried or want to be brave.

Draw Your Growth Mindset Symbol
Draw something that reminds you of being strong and brave , maybe a small plant growing, a superhero, or a sun shining bright!
Remember: Every challenge is a chance to grow. Keep praying, keep believing, and watch yourself get stronger every day!

Therefore I tell you, whatever you ask for in prayer, believe that you have received it, and it will be yours. - Mark 11:24

_____

_____

_____

_____

_____

_____

_____

_____

_____

_____

_____

_____

_____

_____

_____

_____

Therefore I tell you, whatever you ask for in prayer, believe that you
have received it, and it will be yours. - Mark 11:24

Therefore I tell you, whatever you ask for in prayer, believe that you have received it, and it will be yours. - Mark 11:24

Therefore I tell you, whatever you ask for in prayer, believe that you have received it, and it will be yours. - Mark 11:24

Express Yourself

Therefore I tell you, whatever you ask for in prayer, believe that you have received it, and it will be yours. - Mark 11:24

Express Yourself

Therefore I tell you, whatever you ask for in prayer, believe that you have received it, and it will be yours. - Mark 11:24

100

Express Yourself

_____

_____

_____

_____

_____

_____

_____

_____

_____

_____

_____

_____

_____

_____

_____

_____

Therefore I tell you, whatever you ask for in prayer, believe that you have received it, and it will be yours. - Mark 11:24